PUNTA CANA

21 THINGS TO DO IN 7 DAYS

1. Relax on Bavaro Beach

Bavaro Beach, located in Punta Cana, is a tropical paradise renowned for its powdery white sands and crystal-clear turquoise waters. It's the perfect destination for a day of relaxation and sun-soaked bliss.

How to Get There: From Punta Cana International Airport, Bavaro Beach is just a 30-minute drive away. Many resorts in the area also offer shuttle services to the beach.

Price for Tickets: Bavaro Beach itself is a public beach, so there's no admission fee. However, if you're staying at a resort, access to the beach is usually included in your stay.

What to Do: Spend your day basking in the sun, taking leisurely walks along the shoreline, and enjoying the warm, gentle waves. Beach vendors offer water sports activities like jet skiing and parasailing for an additional fee if you're feeling adventurous. You can also find beachfront bars and restaurants where you can savor delicious Dominican cuisine and tropical drinks.

Duration: You can tailor your visit to your preferences. Whether you're looking for a few hours of sun or a full day of relaxation, Bavaro Beach accommodates all schedules.

Valuable Information: Don't forget to bring sunscreen, a hat, and sunglasses to protect yourself from the sun. It's advisable to carry cash for beachside purchases, and be cautious with your belongings. The best time to visit is in the morning to avoid the midday heat.

Bavaro Beach is the epitome of a Caribbean paradise. Whether you're a sunseeker, water sports enthusiast, or simply want to unwind with your toes in the sand, this beach offers a slice of heaven that will make your Punta Cana vacation truly memorable.

2. Go snorkeling

Snorkeling in Punta Cana is a captivating underwater adventure where you can discover the vibrant marine life and stunning coral reefs of the Caribbean Sea.

How to Get There: Most snorkeling tours depart from popular beaches in Punta Cana, such as Bavaro Beach or Cabeza de Toro. Tour operators usually provide transportation to and from your hotel.

Price for Tickets: Snorkeling excursions vary in price but typically range from $50 to $100 per person. Prices often include equipment rental and guides.

What to Do: After a short boat ride to the snorkeling site, you'll be provided with snorkeling gear (mask, snorkel, fins) and receive safety instructions. Then, plunge into the clear, warm waters to explore coral gardens teeming with colorful fish, sea turtles, and other marine creatures. Knowledgeable guides will point out interesting species and ensure your safety throughout the adventure.

Duration: A typical snorkeling excursion lasts around 2 to 3 hours, including travel time to and from your hotel. This allows for plenty of time to explore the underwater world.

Valuable Information:
- Wear sunscreen, a swimsuit, and a rash guard for sun protection.
- Be mindful of the coral reefs; avoid touching or stepping on them to protect the fragile ecosystem.
- If you're new to snorkeling, don't worry; guides will offer assistance and support.
- Bring an underwater camera to capture the mesmerizing marine life.

Snorkeling in Punta Cana offers a unique opportunity to connect with the natural beauty of the Caribbean Sea. Whether you're an experienced snorkeler or a beginner, this activity promises an unforgettable encounter with the underwater wonders of the Dominican Republic.

3. Take a catamaran cruise

A catamaran cruise in Punta Cana is a delightful journey along the picturesque coastline, offering a mix of relaxation, adventure, and tropical beauty. It's a perfect way to experience the Caribbean Sea.

How to Get There: Catamaran cruises usually depart from popular beach areas like Bavaro Beach or Cap Cana. Your tour operator will typically arrange transportation from your hotel to the departure point.

Price for Tickets: The cost of a catamaran cruise can vary depending on the operator, duration, and included amenities. Prices generally range from $70 to $150 per person and may include snorkeling equipment, open bars, and lunch.

What to Do: Once aboard the spacious catamaran, you'll embark on a scenic journey along the coast. Enjoy the refreshing sea breeze, soak up the sun on the deck, and take in stunning views. Most cruises offer opportunities for swimming and snorkeling in pristine waters. You can also relish a delicious lunch served on board, often featuring fresh seafood and tropical fruits. Some cruises include entertainment like music and dancing.

Duration: Catamaran cruises typically last from 3 to 5 hours, depending on the specific tour you choose. This provides ample time for sailing, snorkeling, and relaxation.
Valuable Information:
- Bring swimwear, a towel, sunscreen, and a hat for sun protection.
- If you're prone to seasickness, consider taking motion sickness medication beforehand.
- Respect the environment by not littering and following the guide's instructions during snorkeling.
- Keep valuables secure and waterproof during the trip.

A catamaran cruise in Punta Cana is a fantastic way to experience the beauty of the Dominican coastline and the Caribbean Sea. It offers a blend of relaxation and adventure that's suitable for families, couples, and solo travelers alike. Don't forget your camera to capture the breathtaking moments of your journey.

4. Visit Saona Island

Saona Island is a postcard-perfect tropical paradise located off the southeastern coast of the Dominican Republic. It's renowned for its pristine beaches, crystal-clear waters, and lush palm trees, making it a must-visit destination for nature lovers and beach enthusiasts.

How to Get There: To reach Saona Island, you'll typically need to book a day trip through a tour operator. The journey begins with a bus ride to Bayahibe, followed by a scenic boat ride to the island.

Price for Tickets: The cost of a Saona Island day trip varies but generally ranges from $60 to $100 per person. This usually includes transportation, lunch, and activities.

What to Do: Upon arrival at Saona Island, you'll have the opportunity to relax on the pristine beaches, swim in the azure waters, and enjoy the tranquility of this natural paradise. Many tours also include activities such as beach volleyball, merengue dancing, and beachcombing. You can also explore the island's protected nature reserve, which is home to diverse bird species and mangrove forests.

Duration: A typical Saona Island day trip lasts about 8 to 10 hours, with the majority of your time spent on the island. This allows for ample relaxation and exploration.

Valuable Information:

- Pack essentials like sunscreen, swimwear, a towel, and a hat.
- Protect the fragile ecosystem by not disturbing wildlife or collecting shells and coral.
- Enjoy a buffet lunch with local specialties.
- Be mindful of the sun; it can be quite intense, so reapply sunscreen regularly.
- Keep your belongings secure during the boat ride.

Saona Island is a breathtaking natural wonder that offers a serene escape from the hustle and bustle of Punta Cana. It's a perfect destination for anyone seeking a day of relaxation, beachcombing, and natural beauty in the Dominican Republic. Be sure to have your camera ready to capture the stunning scenery and memories of this idyllic island.

5. Explore Hoyo Azul

Hoyo Azul, meaning "Blue Hole," is a mesmerizing natural cenote located within the Scape Park at Cap Cana. It's a unique geological formation, characterized by its stunning turquoise water surrounded by lush tropical forest.

How to Get There: To reach Hoyo Azul, you'll need to visit Scape Park, which is about a 20 to 30-minute drive from most Punta Cana resorts. You can arrange transportation through the park or use a taxi.

Price for Tickets: The entrance fee to Scape Park, which includes access to Hoyo Azul, varies depending on the package and activities you choose. Prices typically range from $90 to $150 per person.

What to Do: Upon arriving at Scape Park, you'll take a guided nature walk through the jungle to reach Hoyo Azul. The walk is a part of the experience, allowing you to admire the local flora and fauna. When you arrive at Hoyo Azul, you can take a refreshing dip in the cool, crystal-clear water of the cenote. The experience is both relaxing and exhilarating as you swim in the stunning blue waters surrounded by lush greenery. Don't forget your camera; the vivid colors of Hoyo Azul make for stunning photos.

Duration: The entire experience, including the guided walk to and from Hoyo Azul, typically takes around 2 to 3 hours. This allows you to fully enjoy the natural beauty of the cenote.
Valuable Information:
- Wear comfortable walking shoes, swimwear, and a towel.
- Sunscreen is essential, as parts of the walk to Hoyo Azul can be sunny.
- Respect the natural environment by not leaving any litter behind.
- There are changing facilities and lockers available at Scape Park.
- Be cautious on the slippery rocks around the cenote.

Hoyo Azul is a hidden gem in Punta Cana, offering a unique and refreshing adventure in a pristine natural setting. It's a must-visit for nature enthusiasts and anyone seeking a serene escape in the Dominican Republic.

6. Zip line at Scape Park

Zip-lining at Scape Park in Punta Cana offers an exhilarating adventure through lush tropical landscapes, allowing you to soar above the treetops and experience the thrill of flying.

How to Get There: Scape Park is located in the Cap Cana resort area, approximately a 20 to 30-minute drive from most Punta Cana hotels. You can arrange transportation through the park or take a taxi to reach the location.

Price for Tickets: Ticket prices for zip-lining at Scape Park can vary depending on the package and the number of activities you choose to include. Prices generally range from $70 to $130 per person.

What to Do: After arriving at Scape Park, you'll be equipped with safety gear and receive instructions from professional guides. Then, you'll embark on a thrilling zip line adventure, gliding through the canopy of a lush forest. The park offers multiple zip line circuits, including lines that pass over cliffs and natural cenotes. You'll also have opportunities to take in breathtaking views of the surrounding scenery.

Duration: The duration of your zip-lining experience depends on the package you choose and the number of zip lines you decide to ride. On average, this adventure typically takes around 2 to 3 hours, including orientation, equipment setup, and the actual zip-lining.

Valuable Information:
- Wear comfortable clothing and closed-toe shoes suitable for physical activity.
- Bring sunscreen, insect repellent, and a reusable water bottle.
- Follow the safety instructions provided by your guides.
- Scape Park offers other activities, such as swimming in cenotes, cave exploration, and cultural experiences. Consider exploring these options to make the most of your visit.

Zip-lining at Scape Park is a thrilling way to experience the natural beauty of Punta Cana from a unique perspective. Whether you're an adventure enthusiast or seeking an adrenaline rush, this activity is sure to provide an unforgettable experience in the Dominican Republic. Don't forget to capture the breathtaking views on your camera to relive the adventure later.

7. Horseback ride along the beach

Horseback riding along the beach in Punta Cana is a romantic and picturesque adventure, allowing you to explore the stunning coastline on horseback. It's a perfect way to enjoy the natural beauty of the Dominican Republic.

How to Get There: Most horseback riding tours depart from popular beach areas like Bavaro Beach. Tour operators often provide transportation from your hotel to the starting point. Price for Tickets: The cost of a horseback riding tour varies depending on the operator, duration, and whether additional activities are included. Prices generally range from $50 to $100 per person.

What to Do: After arriving at the stables, you'll receive a brief orientation on horseback riding and safety. Then, you'll saddle up and embark on a scenic ride along the beach. You'll have the opportunity to enjoy the gentle ocean breeze, take in the stunning views, and even go for a refreshing swim with your horse. Guides typically accompany the group to ensure safety and provide information about the area.

Duration: A typical horseback ride along the beach in Punta Cana lasts around 1 to 2 hours, depending on the specific tour. This allows for a leisurely exploration of the coastline. Valuable Information:

- Wear comfortable clothing and closed-toe shoes suitable for horseback riding.
- Sunscreen, sunglasses, and a hat are essential for sun protection.
- Follow your guide's instructions to ensure a safe and enjoyable ride.
- Be mindful of your horse's well-being; treat it with care and respect.

Horseback riding along the beach in Punta Cana offers a unique perspective of the stunning coastline and provides an unforgettable experience in the Dominican Republic. Whether you're a beginner or an experienced rider, this activity is suitable for all levels and is perfect for couples and families. Don't forget your camera to capture the beauty of your ride and the breathtaking scenery along the way.

8. Explore Indigenous Eyes Ecological Park

The Indigenous Eyes Ecological Park and Reserve is a hidden gem in Punta Cana, offering a unique natural experience. This privately-owned park is home to lush tropical forests, a series of freshwater lagoons, and diverse wildlife, making it a haven for nature enthusiasts.

How to Get There: Indigenous Eyes Ecological Park is conveniently located in the Punta Cana Resort & Club area. If you're staying at a nearby resort, you can often access the park through guided tours arranged by your hotel. Otherwise, you can take a taxi or arrange transportation through a tour operator.

Price for Tickets: The entrance fee to the park can vary depending on whether you are a resort guest or a non-resort guest. Prices generally range from $25 to $50 per person.

What to Do: Upon entering the park, you can explore a network of well-maintained trails that lead you through lush forests and past several pristine lagoons. The park is named after its 12 freshwater lagoons, locally known as "Ojos Indígenas" (Indigenous Eyes). These lagoons are perfect for swimming and are surrounded by serene natural beauty.

Duration: You can spend as little as 1-2 hours or as much as half a day exploring the Indigenous Eyes Ecological Park, depending on your level of interest and the activities you choose.
Valuable Information:
- Wear comfortable clothing and closed-toe shoes suitable for walking.
- Bring sunscreen, insect repellent, and a reusable water bottle.
- Be respectful of the natural environment; do not litter or disturb wildlife.
- Swimming is allowed in some of the lagoons, so bring swimwear if you plan to take a dip.
- Guided tours are available for a more informative experience.

The Indigenous Eyes Ecological Park offers a serene escape from the bustling tourist areas of Punta Cana. It's a peaceful oasis where you can immerse yourself in the natural beauty of the Dominican Republic and learn about its unique ecosystems. Whether you're a nature lover, a photographer, or simply seeking a tranquil retreat, this park is a must-visit during your trip to Punta Cana.

9. Swim in the Marinarium

The Marinarium in Punta Cana offers a unique opportunity to swim in a natural marine aquarium. It's a fascinating experience where you can interact with marine life and explore the vibrant underwater world of the Caribbean Sea.

How to Get There: The Marinarium is located in the Cabeza de Toro area, approximately a 20 to 30-minute drive from most Punta Cana resorts. You can arrange transportation through the Marinarium or use a taxi to reach the location.

Price for Tickets: Ticket prices for the Marinarium vary depending on the package and activities you choose. Prices generally range from $100 to $150 per person. Most packages include snorkeling equipment, a boat trip, and refreshments.

What to Do: Your Marinarium adventure begins with a boat ride to a floating platform in the middle of the ocean, where you'll be provided with snorkeling gear. Once in the water, you can swim alongside nurse sharks and stingrays in their natural habitat. The experience is safe and guided by marine experts who offer valuable insights about these incredible creatures. Afterward, you'll snorkel in a coral reef area teeming with colorful fish and other marine life. Youcan also relax on the platform, bask in the sun, and enjoy drinks and snacks.

Duration: A typical Marinarium excursion takes around 3 to 4 hours, including transportation to and from your hotel. This provides ample time for snorkeling, swimming, and relaxation.
Valuable Information:

- Wear swimwear, sunscreen, and a hat for sun protection.
- Listen to the guides' instructions for safe interaction with the marine life.
- Bring an underwater camera to capture your underwater adventure.
- Be cautious with your belongings and use provided lockers for storage.
- The Marinarium is suitable for all ages and swimming levels.

Swimming in the Marinarium is a thrilling and educational experience that allows you to get up close and personal with some of the Caribbean's most fascinating marine species. Whether you're a snorkeling enthusiast or a first-time snorkeler, this adventure promises unforgettable moments in the Dominican Republic's underwater world.

10. Go on a dune buggy adventure

A dune buggy adventure in Punta Cana is an adrenaline-packed excursion that combines off-roading thrills with exploring the rugged terrain of the Dominican Republic. It's an exciting way to discover the region's natural beauty.

How to Get There: Most dune buggy tours offer hotel pickup, making it convenient for tourists. After being picked up from your hotel, you'll typically be taken to the starting point of the adventure.

Price for Tickets: The cost of a dune buggy adventure varies based on the operator, the duration of the tour, and any additional inclusions. Prices generally range from $80 to $150 per person.

What to Do: Once you arrive at the starting point, you'll receive a safety briefing and be provided with a helmet and goggles. Then, you'll hop into a dune buggy and follow a guide through rugged terrain, including dirt trails, muddy paths, and scenic countryside. You'll pass by local villages, stop at a beach for a swim, and explore areas off the beaten path. Many tours include opportunities for a refreshing dip in a cenote (natural sinkhole) or a cave.

Duration: A typical dune buggy adventure in Punta Cana lasts around 3 to 4 hours, including transportation to and from your hotel. This allows for an exhilarating and immersive experience. Valuable Information:

- Dress in comfortable clothing that can get dirty, and wear closed-toe shoes.
- Apply sunscreen generously, as you'll be exposed to the sun during the ride.
- Bring a change of clothes if you plan to swim.
- Follow your guide's instructions for safe dune buggy operation.
- Keep your belongings secure during the ride.

A dune buggy adventure in Punta Cana offers an exciting mix of off-road exploration and natural beauty. It's suitable for adventure enthusiasts and those looking to experience the Dominican Republic's countryside in an unconventional way. Don't forget to bring your camera to capture the scenic landscapes and thrilling moments along the way.

11. Visit Altos de Chavón

Altos de Chavón is a charming, replica Mediterranean village nestled along the Chavón River in the Dominican Republic. This cultural and artistic center offers visitors a unique blend of history, art, and breathtaking architecture.

How to Get There: Altos de Chavón is located in the Casa de Campo resort area, about an hour's drive from Punta Cana. Most visitors arrange transportation through tour operators or their hotels. Taxis are also readily available.

Price for Tickets: The entrance fee to Altos de Chavón varies but generally ranges from $20 to $30 per person. This typically includes access to the village and its attractions.

What to Do: Once you arrive at Altos de Chavón, you'll be transported to a charming 16th-century Mediterranean village. Explore cobblestone streets, admire the stunning architecture, and visit attractions like the St. Stanislaus Church, the Regional Museum of Archaeology, and the Art Gallery. Don't miss the opportunity to see local artisans at work, creating beautiful handicrafts. Enjoy panoramic views of the Chavón River and its surrounding landscapes. You can also savor Dominican and international cuisine at the village's restaurants.

Duration: A visit to Altos de Chavón can take approximately 2 to 3 hours, depending on your level of interest in exploring the village's attractions and taking in the views.
Valuable Information:

- Wear comfortable walking shoes and lightweight clothing.
- Bring sunscreen, a hat, and a camera to capture the picturesque scenery.
- Respect the cultural and historical significance of the village.
- Some attractions may have additional entrance fees, so check before entering.
- Altos de Chavón occasionally hosts live performances and cultural events, so consider checking the schedule for special experiences.

Altos de Chavón offers a delightful change of pace from Punta Cana's beaches and water adventures. It's a place where history, art, and Dominican culture come together in a picturesque setting. Whether you're interested in history, art, or simply enjoying a leisurely stroll, this charming village is a must-visit during your stay in Punta Cana.

12. Try parasailing

Parasailing in Punta Cana is a thrilling water sport that allows you to soar high above the sparkling Caribbean Sea while being towed by a boat. It offers a unique perspective of the stunning coastline and clear waters.

How to Get There: Parasailing operators are usually located on popular beaches like Bavaro Beach and Cortecito Beach in Punta Cana. You can easily access these locations from most resorts in the area, either by a short walk or a quick taxi ride.

Price for Tickets: The cost of parasailing in Punta Cana can vary based on factors such as location, duration, and package inclusions. Prices generally range from $50 to $100 per person. What to Do: Your parasailing adventure begins with a safety briefing by trained professionals. You'll be fitted with a harness and life jacket. After that, you'll board a speedboat, and as it gains momentum, you'll gradually ascend into the air while securely attached to a parachute. Once airborne, you'll enjoy breathtaking panoramic views of the coastline and the turquoise Caribbean waters. You can choose to parasail solo or in tandem with a friend.

Duration: A typical parasailing experience in Punta Cana lasts around 10 to 15 minutes, but this can vary depending on the package and operator. The entire activity, including safety instructions and boat transport, usually takes around 30 minutes to an hour.
Valuable Information:
- Wear swimwear or comfortable clothing suitable for water activities.
- Apply sunscreen generously, as you'll be exposed to the sun.
- Cameras are often not allowed during the flight, but operators typically offer photo and video packages for purchase.
- Listen to your guide's instructions for a safe and enjoyable experience.
- Parasailing is generally suitable for individuals of all ages, but weight and age restrictions may apply.

Parasailing in Punta Cana is a thrilling adventure that provides a unique opportunity to experience the beauty of the Dominican coastline from the sky. It's an exhilarating water activity suitable for couples, families, and solo travelers alike. Don't forget to bring your sense of adventure and a smile for the stunning views you'll enjoy during your flight.

13. Go kiteboarding

Kiteboarding in Punta Cana is an exciting water sport that combines elements of windsurfing, wakeboarding, and paragliding. It involves harnessing the power of the wind to propel yourself across the water on a small board.

How to Get There: Most kiteboarding centers in Punta Cana are located along the coastline, particularly in areas like Cabarete and La Boca. You can arrange transportation through the kiteboarding center or take a taxi to reach your chosen location.

Price for Tickets: The cost of kiteboarding lessons or rentals can vary depending on factors like the duration of your lesson, the type of equipment you need, and the kiteboarding center you choose. Prices generally range from $50 for a basic lesson to $150 or more for a full-day package.

What to Do: Your kiteboarding adventure begins with a safety briefing and an introduction to the equipment. You'll learn about kite control, safety measures, and how to handle the kite. Then, you'll take to the water under the guidance of a certified instructor. During your lesson, you'll practice launching and controlling the kite, body dragging through the water, and eventually, riding the board. Kiteboarding is an adrenaline-pumping experience that combines skill, balance, and the thrill of harnessing the wind's power.

Duration: The duration of your kiteboarding experience can vary based on the lesson package you choose. A typical lesson lasts around 2 to 3 hours, including setup, instruction, and practice time. Valuable Information:

- Wear swimwear or a wetsuit, depending on the water temperature.
- Apply sunscreen generously to protect your skin from the sun and water reflection.
- Be prepared for physical activity; kiteboarding can be physically demanding.
- Follow your instructor's guidance carefully for safety and optimal learning.
- Kiteboarding is generally suitable for individuals who are comfortable in the water and in good physical condition.

Kiteboarding in Punta Cana is an exhilarating way to experience the thrill of the Caribbean Sea and the power of the wind. Whether you're a seasoned kiteboarder or a beginner looking to learn, there are options for everyone.

12. Play golf at Punta Espada Golf Course

Punta Espada Golf Course is a world-class golfing destination in Punta Cana, renowned for its stunning seaside location, challenging layout, and impeccable conditions. It's designed by the legendary golfer Jack Nicklaus and offers an exceptional golfing experience in the Dominican Republic.

How to Get There: Punta Espada Golf Course is located in the Cap Cana resort area, approximately a 20 to 30-minute drive from most Punta Cana hotels. Transportation is often arranged through the golf course or your hotel.

Price for Tickets: The cost of playing at Punta Espada can vary depending on the season, time of day, and any additional services included (such as caddy and golf cart). Prices generally range from $200 to $350 per round. Discounts may be available for resort guests and during certain times of the year.

What to Do: Playing golf at Punta Espada is an exceptional experience. The course features 18 holes with spectacular ocean views, challenging fairways, and lush greens. Enjoy the refreshing sea breeze as you navigate through this championship course. The clubhouse offers a luxurious setting for pre-game preparations and post-game relaxation.

Duration: A round of golf at Punta Espada can take approximately 4 to 5 hours, depending on your skill level and pace of play. Factor in additional time for arrival, preparation, and post-round relaxation. Valuable Information:

- Wear proper golf attire, including collared shirts and soft-spiked golf shoes.
- Reserve your tee time in advance, especially during peak seasons.
- Check the golf course's dress code and rules, including pace of play.
- Golf club rentals and golf instruction are often available for those who don't bring their clubs or want to improve their game.
- Respect the course and keep pace with the group ahead of you.

Punta Espada Golf Course offers a world-class golfing experience in one of the most beautiful settings in the Dominican Republic.

15. Explore the Manati Park

Manati Park is a captivating wildlife and cultural theme park in Punta Cana. It's a family-friendly destination where you can discover a diverse range of animals, enjoy live entertainment, and immerse yourself in the Dominican Republic's rich culture.

How to Get There: Manati Park is conveniently located in the Bavaro area of Punta Cana, making it easily accessible by taxi or shuttle from most nearby resorts. Many hotels also offer guided tours to the park.

Price for Tickets: The cost of admission to Manati Park can vary depending on age and any additional activities or packages you choose. Prices generally range from $20 to $50 per person, with discounts often available for children.

What to Do: Upon entering Manati Park, you'll embark on a journey through its lush tropical setting. You can interact with a variety of animals, including dolphins, sea lions, parrots, and iguanas. The park offers entertaining live shows featuring these animals, providing educational insights into their behavior and habitats. Additionally, you'll have the opportunity to explore beautiful botanical gardens and observe indigenous Taino culture, with reenactments and art exhibitions.

Duration: A visit to Manati Park typically takes around 2 to 3 hours, but you can choose to spend more time enjoying the shows, exploring the gardens, or interacting with the animals. Valuable Information:

- Wear comfortable clothing and walking shoes suitable for exploring the park.
- Apply sunscreen and insect repellent, as you'll be outdoors.
- Follow park rules and guidelines for respectful animal interactions.
- Photography is allowed; consider bringing a camera to capture memorable moments.
- Manati Park offers dining options and gift shops for souvenirs.

Manati Park is a delightful place to experience the biodiversity and culture of the Dominican Republic in a single visit. It's particularly well-suited for families and animal enthusiasts. The educational shows and hands-on encounters with wildlife make it an engaging and memorable day trip option in Punta Cana.

16. Discover Indigenous Art Museum

The Indigenous Art Museum in Punta Cana is a cultural treasure trove dedicated to preserving and showcasing the rich heritage and artistry of the Dominican Republic's indigenous Taino people. It's a fascinating journey into the history, art, and traditions of this ancient civilization.

How to Get There: The Indigenous Art Museum is situated within the Punta Cana Resort & Club complex, making it easily accessible from many hotels in the area. You can arrange transportation through the museum or your hotel. It's a short drive from most Punta Cana resorts.

Price for Tickets: The entrance fee to the Indigenous Art Museum is typically very affordable, ranging from $5 to $10 per person. Children and seniors often receive discounted rates.

What to Do: Upon arriving at the museum, you'll step into a world that transports you back in time to the Taino culture. Explore an extensive collection of artifacts, pottery, sculptures, and artwork that provide insights into the daily life and spirituality of the Taino people. Knowledgeable guides are available to offer explanations and answer questions. You can also enjoy cultural demonstrations, art exhibitions, and workshops that celebrate the Taino heritage. The museum's serene surroundings, including lush gardens and scenic views, offer a peaceful backdrop for your visit.

Duration: A visit to the Indigenous Art Museum typically takes around 1 to 2 hours, allowing ample time to explore the exhibits and immerse yourself in the Taino culture.

Valuable Information:

- Wear comfortable walking shoes and lightweight clothing.
- Bring sunscreen and insect repellent if you plan to explore the outdoor areas.
- Photography is often allowed, but inquire about specific rules and restrictions.
- Support local artisans by considering the purchase of Taino-inspired crafts and artwork available at the museum.
- Respect the cultural significance of the exhibits and artifacts.

The Indigenous Art Museum in Punta Cana offers a unique opportunity to learn about and appreciate the heritage of the Dominican Republic's indigenous people.

17. Take a helicopter tour

A helicopter tour in Punta Cana offers a thrilling and scenic perspective of the Dominican Republic's stunning landscapes, including pristine beaches, lush jungles, and crystal-clear waters. It's a unique way to capture the beauty of this tropical paradise from the sky.

How to Get There: Helicopter tour operators in Punta Cana are typically based at the Punta Cana International Airport or nearby helipads. Most operators offer hotel pickup services, making it convenient for tourists. You can also choose to drive to the departure location or take a taxi.

Price for Tickets: The cost of a helicopter tour can vary depending on the length of the tour, the route, and the operator. Prices generally range from $100 to $300 per person for a short tour, while longer, more comprehensive tours may cost more.

What to Do: Your helicopter tour begins with a safety briefing and an introduction to the aircraft. Once you're in the air, you'll enjoy breathtaking panoramic views of Punta Cana's coastline, beaches, resorts, and natural landmarks like the Hoyo Azul cenote. Professional pilots provide informative commentary throughout the tour, pointing out key points of interest and sharing local knowledge. Be sure to bring your camera or smartphone to capture the incredible views.

Duration: The duration of a helicopter tour can vary depending on the route chosen. Short tours typically last around 15 to 20 minutes, while longer tours can extend to 45 minutes or more.
Valuable Information:

- Wear comfortable clothing and bring sunglasses to protect your eyes from the sun's glare.
- Be punctual and arrive at the departure location on time.
- Listen to the pilot's instructions and remain seated during the flight.
- Helicopter tours are generally suitable for all ages, but check with the operator for specific age and weight restrictions.
- Consider the weight and balance restrictions when booking; some operators may require you to disclose your weight in advance.

A helicopter tour in Punta Cana offers a breathtaking experience that allows you to see the Dominican Republic's natural beauty from a unique vantage point.

18. Go on a fishing excursion

A fishing excursion in Punta Cana offers an opportunity to experience the thrill of deep-sea fishing in the Caribbean Sea. Whether you're a seasoned angler or a beginner, you can enjoy a day of adventure on the water, aiming to catch a variety of fish species.

How to Get There: Most fishing excursions depart from marinas in the Punta Cana area, such as the Marina Cap Cana. These marinas are easily accessible from most Punta Cana resorts, and transportation is often included in the excursion package.

Price for Tickets: The cost of a fishing excursion in Punta Cana varies depending on factors like the type of fishing (deep-sea or inshore), the duration of the trip, and the charter operator. Prices generally range from $150 to $400 per person. The cost typically includes fishing equipment, bait, and refreshments.

What to Do: Your fishing adventure begins with a boat ride from the marina to prime fishing spots offshore. Professional guides and crew members provide instruction and assistance throughout the trip. You'll have the chance to catch a variety of fish species, including marlin, dorado, wahoo, and snapper. Most fishing excursions offer catch-and-release policies to preserve the local fish populations, but some allow you to keep your catch. Enjoy the thrill of reeling in your fish and take in the stunning views of the Caribbean Sea.

Duration: A typical fishing excursion in Punta Cana can last from 4 to 8 hours, depending on the package you choose. This allows for a comprehensive fishing experience and the opportunity to explore various fishing grounds.

Valuable Information:
- Wear comfortable clothing and a hat to protect yourself from the sun.
- Apply sunscreen generously, as you'll be exposed to the sun for an extended period.
- Many fishing charters provide snacks and drinks, but you can bring additional items if you prefer.
- Be prepared for sea conditions, as the Caribbean waters can sometimes be choppy.

A fishing excursion in Punta Cana is an exciting adventure that caters to both experienced anglers and beginners. It's a fantastic way to enjoy the beauty of the Caribbean Sea while trying your hand at a rewarding sport.

19. Visit Macao Beach

Macao Beach is a picturesque and unspoiled stretch of shoreline located on the east coast of Punta Cana. Known for its pristine beauty, it offers a tranquil escape from the resort areas, making it a perfect destination for beach lovers and nature enthusiasts.

How to Get There: Macao Beach is easily accessible from Punta Cana resorts by taxi or guided tours. It's approximately a 20 to 30-minute drive from the popular tourist areas, and the journey itself offers scenic views of the countryside.

Price for Tickets: There is typically no entrance fee to visit Macao Beach. However, if you choose to join a guided tour that includes additional activities or services, such as water sports or horseback riding, there may be associated costs.

What to Do: At Macao Beach, you can indulge in various activities or simply relax and enjoy the natural beauty. Some popular activities include swimming in the turquoise waters, sunbathing on the soft, golden sands, and taking long walks along the shoreline. The beach is also favored by surfers, thanks to its consistent waves. Local vendors may offer horseback riding excursions, surf lessons, or snacks and refreshments.

Duration: The length of your visit to Macao Beach can vary based on your interests. You can spend a few hours sunbathing and swimming or opt for a full-day adventure if you decide to explore the nearby attractions. Valuable Information:

- Wear swimwear or beach attire, and don't forget sunscreen and sunglasses.
- Be mindful of ocean currents and waves, especially if you plan to swim or surf.
- Support local businesses by trying traditional Dominican dishes or purchasing handmade crafts.
- Respect the natural environment by disposing of trash properly and not disturbing wildlife.
- If you opt for guided tours, check the itinerary for additional inclusions like lunch or activities.

Macao Beach is a hidden gem in Punta Cana, offering a peaceful retreat from the bustling resort areas. Whether you seek relaxation, water sports, or a taste of local culture, this beach has something for every traveler. It's an excellent spot to unwind, soak up the sun, and experience the unspoiled beauty of the Dominican Republic's coastline.

20. Experience Scape to Cap Cana

Scape to Cap Cana is a unique entertainment and adventure complex located in the upscale Cap Cana resort area of Punta Cana. It offers a diverse range of activities, from zip-lining and horseback riding to beachfront relaxation and dining, making it an ideal destination for a day of fun and exploration.

How to Get There: Scape to Cap Cana is situated in the Cap Cana resort area, about a 20 to 30-minute drive from most Punta Cana hotels. Many hotels offer transportation services, or you can arrange a taxi to take you there.

Price for Tickets: The cost of admission to Scape to Cap Cana varies based on the activities and experiences you choose to include. Prices can range from $50 for basic packages to $200 or more for full-day experiences with multiple activities.

What to Do: Scape to Cap Cana offers a wide array of activities to suit all interests. You can start your day with thrilling zip-lining adventures over lush forests, followed by horseback riding along pristine beaches. The complex also features a beautiful infinity pool and a private beach area, perfect for sunbathing and relaxation. Dining options include a beach club and restaurants where you can savor local and international cuisine. For water enthusiasts, there are opportunities for snorkeling, paddleboarding, and kayaking.

Duration: A visit to Scape to Cap Cana can last anywhere from a few hours to a full day, depending on the activities and experiences you choose to enjoy. Valuable Information:

- Wear comfortable clothing suitable for outdoor activities, including swimwear if you plan to swim or enjoy water sports.
- Apply sunscreen generously to protect your skin from the sun.
- Bring a change of clothes if you participate in water activities.
- Listen to the guides' instructions for safety and enjoyment during adventures.
- Make reservations for popular activities in advance, especially during peak tourist seasons.

Scape to Cap Cana is a versatile destination that caters to a wide range of interests, making it a fantastic choice for families, couples, and groups of friends. Whether you're seeking adventure, relaxation, or a bit of both, this complex has something to offer. Don't forget your camera to capture the thrilling moments and stunning views during your Scape to Cap Cana experience.

21. Enjoy nightlife at Coco Bongo Punta Cana

Coco Bongo is a renowned nightclub and entertainment venue in Punta Cana, known for its electrifying nightlife experience. It combines music, dance, acrobatics, and stunning visuals to create an unforgettable party atmosphere.

How to Get There: Coco Bongo Punta Cana is located in the Downtown Punta Cana area. If you're staying in a nearby resort, many offer transportation services to and from the club. Alternatively, you can arrange for a taxi to take you there.

Price for Tickets: The cost of admission to Coco Bongo can vary depending on factors like the day of the week, the type of ticket, and any additional inclusions (such as VIP access or open bar). Prices generally range from $60 to $150 per person.

What to Do: Coco Bongo offers a high-energy, immersive experience. The night typically begins with a spectacular pre-show featuring acrobats, dancers, and impersonators. Once the main party starts, you can dance the night away to a mix of music genres played by talented DJs and a live band. Enjoy performances that include flying acrobats, confetti showers, and visual effects that transport you to different worlds. The club often hosts theme nights and special events, adding even more excitement to the experience.

Duration: A night at Coco Bongo typically lasts from 10:30 PM to around 3:30 AM. It's an all-night party, so pace yourself to make the most of the experience. Valuable Information:
- Dress code is typically smart casual; avoid wearing beachwear or flip-flops.
- You must be at least 18 years old to enter Coco Bongo.
- Make reservations in advance, especially if you want VIP access or specific table arrangements.
- Arrive early to secure a good spot, as the club can get crowded.
- Be mindful of your belongings and personal safety in crowded spaces.

Coco Bongo Punta Cana offers an electrifying nightlife experience that's perfect for those seeking a memorable night out. It's a popular spot for groups, couples, and friends looking to dance, be entertained, and create lasting memories.

When visiting Punta Cana here are 7 valuable pieces of advice to keep in mind:

1. Sun Protection: The Caribbean sun can be intense. Always wear sunscreen with a high SPF, sunglasses, and a wide-brimmed hat to protect yourself from sunburn.

2. Stay Hydrated: It's easy to get dehydrated in the tropical climate. Drink plenty of bottled water, especially if you're enjoying outdoor activities or spending time at the beach.

3. Respect the Environment: Keep Punta Cana's natural beauty intact by disposing of trash responsibly and respecting the local flora and fauna. Avoid touching or disturbing coral reefs if you go snorkeling.

4. Currency: The local currency is the Dominican Peso (DOP), but US dollars are widely accepted. However, it's a good idea to carry some local currency for smaller purchases and to avoid unfavorable exchange rates.

5. Learn Basic Spanish: While many people in the tourism industry speak English, learning a few basic Spanish phrases can be helpful and appreciated by the locals.

6. Negotiate Prices: When shopping in local markets or hiring services like taxis, it's often expected that you'll negotiate the price. Be prepared to haggle a bit to get a fair deal.

7. Safety: Like any travel destination, be mindful of your personal belongings, especially in crowded areas. Use hotel safes for valuables and avoid walking alone at night in unfamiliar areas.

Remember that Punta Cana is a popular tourist destination known for its warm and friendly atmosphere. By being respectful of the local culture and environment and taking some basic precautions, you can have a safe and enjoyable visit.

Here are 7 of the best services to consider using:

1. Airport Transfers: Arrange for airport transportation in advance to ensure a hassle-free arrival and departure. Many hotels offer shuttle services, or you can book private transfers for added convenience.

2. Tour and Excursion Operators: Utilize reputable tour and excursion operators to explore the area's attractions. Whether it's snorkeling, zip-lining, or cultural tours, these operators provide guided experiences to make the most of your visit.

3. Beach Clubs: Spend a relaxing day at one of Punta Cana's beach clubs. These venues offer amenities like sun loungers, beachside service, and water sports equipment, allowing you to unwind in style.

4. Local Guides: Consider hiring a local guide when exploring off-the-beaten-path destinations or learning about the region's culture and history. Guides can provide valuable insights and enrich your experience.

5. Spa and Wellness Services: Pamper yourself with spa treatments at your resort or at standalone wellness centers. Many offer massages, facials, and holistic therapies to help you relax and rejuvenate.

6. Golf Courses: Punta Cana boasts world-class golf courses. If you're a golfer, make use of the services offered by these courses, from club rentals to expert instruction.

7. Nightlife Entertainment: Experience the vibrant nightlife by booking tickets or VIP packages at popular clubs and entertainment venues like Coco Bongo. These services often include transportation, reserved seating, and other perks.

By utilizing these services, you can enhance your Punta Cana vacation and ensure that you make the most of your time in this beautiful destination. Whether you're seeking relaxation, adventure, or entertainment, there are services available to suit your preferences.

Top 7 Must-Try Dining Spots in Punta Cana:

1. La Yola Restaurant: Located at the Punta Cana Marina, La Yola offers a unique dining experience right on the water. Enjoy fresh seafood and Mediterranean-inspired dishes while taking in marina views.

2. Jellyfish Restaurant: This beachfront eatery is known for its seafood dishes, including a variety of ceviches. The romantic ambiance and live music make it a popular spot for couples.

3. Balicana Asian Cuisine: If you're in the mood for Asian flavors, Balicana is a top choice. The menu features dishes from across Asia, including sushi, Thai curries, and Vietnamese pho.

4. Passion by Martin Berasategui: Located within the Paradisus Palma Real Resort, this Michelin-starred restaurant offers a gourmet dining experience with a focus on contemporary Spanish cuisine.

5. Huracán Café: Situated right on Bavaro Beach, Huracán Café offers a mix of international and Dominican dishes. It's known for its lobster and seafood, served in a beachfront, thatched-roof setting.

6. Captain Cook Restaurant: This seafood restaurant is a hidden gem in Punta Cana. It's a local favorite known for its flavorful shrimp dishes and relaxed atmosphere.

7. Bamboo Restaurant: Located at the Now Larimar Punta Cana Resort, Bamboo serves a fusion of Asian and Peruvian cuisine. Sushi lovers will appreciate the creative rolls and fresh sashimi.

These dining spots offer a range of culinary experiences, from upscale dining to casual beachfront eateries. Whether you're a seafood enthusiast, an adventurous foodie, or simply looking for a romantic dinner with a view, Punta Cana's dining scene has something to satisfy every palate.

Here are 7 crucial phone numbers to know:

1. Emergency Services: In case of emergencies, dial **911**. This number connects you to the local emergency services, including police, medical assistance, and fire.

2. Tourist Police: The Tourist Police in Punta Cana can assist tourists with various issues, including reporting theft or seeking help in emergencies. Their number is often listed as **809-552-0987**.

3. U.S. Embassy or Consulate: If you're a U.S. citizen, it's wise to have the contact information for the nearest U.S. Embassy or Consulate. The U.S. Embassy in Santo Domingo can be reached at **+1 809-567-7775**.

4. Local Hospital: Know the contact information for the nearest hospital in case of medical emergencies. The Hospiten Bavaro is a well-known hospital in the Punta Cana area, and their emergency line is **+1 809-686-1414**.

5. Taxi Service: Save the number of a reputable taxi service in your area, as you may need transportation during your stay. Be cautious with unlicensed taxi drivers.

6. Resort or Hotel Front Desk: Keep the front desk number of your resort or hotel handy for any questions or assistance you may need during your stay.

7. Airport Information: If you need to check flight details, inquire about lost luggage, or seek airport assistance, have the contact information for the Punta Cana International Airport. Their general information line is **+1 809-959-2376**.

Having these essential phone numbers readily available can help ensure your safety and provide assistance when needed during your visit to Punta Cana.

7 unknown facts about Punta Cana:

1. Golf Paradise: Punta Cana is a golf lover's paradise. It boasts several world-class golf courses designed by renowned architects, making it a top destination for golf enthusiasts. The Punta Espada Golf Course, designed by Jack Nicklaus, is particularly famous and has been a host to prestigious tournaments.

2. Coral Reefs: While Punta Cana is known for its beautiful beaches, it's also home to vibrant coral reefs. The underwater world here is teeming with marine life, making it an excellent spot for snorkeling and scuba diving. Check out spots like Catalina Island and Isla Saona for fantastic underwater experiences.

3. Coconut Coast: Punta Cana is often referred to as the "Coconut Coast" because of the abundance of coconut palms lining its pristine beaches. You can enjoy fresh coconut water or even sample local dishes made with coconut in many restaurants.

4. Higuey Basilica: Just a short drive from Punta Cana, you'll find the town of Higuey, home to the Basilica of Our Lady of Altagracia. This stunning basilica is a significant pilgrimage site and one of the most important religious landmarks in the Dominican Republic.

5. Chocolate and Cigars: The Dominican Republic is famous for its cocoa production. In Punta Cana, you can visit local cacao plantations and learn about the chocolate-making process.

6. Indigenous Taino Culture: The Dominican Republic has a rich history, and Punta Cana is no exception. The area was once inhabited by the indigenous Taino people, and you can learn about their culture and history at the Indigenous Eyes Ecological Park & Reserve.

7. Hoyo Azul: Tucked away in the Scape Park, you'll find Hoyo Azul, a stunning natural cenote. Its name means "Blue Hole," and it's famous for its incredibly clear, blue water. You can swim in this refreshing cenote and enjoy the surrounding lush vegetation.

These lesser-known facts add depth to Punta Cana's appeal, highlighting its diverse offerings beyond its beautiful beaches. Whether you're interested in history, outdoor adventures, or culinary experiences, Punta Cana has something unique to offer.

Printed in Great Britain
by Amazon

45730819R00020